WIN THE
MEN

WIN THE MEN

30 Day Journey

J.K. GOODSON

Win the Men

Copyright © 2021 by J.K. Goodson. All rights reserved.

No part of this publication may be reproduced, stored in a retrieval system or transmitted in any way by any means, electronic, mechanical, photocopy, recording or otherwise without the prior permission of the author except as provided by USA copyright law.

The opinions expressed by the author are not necessarily those of URLink Print and Media.

1603 Capitol Ave., Suite 310 Cheyenne, Wyoming USA 82001
1-888-980-6523 | admin@urlinkpublishing.com

URLink Print and Media is committed to excellence in the publishing industry.

Book design copyright © 2021 by URLink Print and Media. All rights reserved.

Published in the United States of America
ISBN 978-1-64753-596-4 (Paperback)
ISBN 978-1-64753-597-1 (Hardback)
ISBN 978-1-64753-598-8 (Digital)

20.11.20

CONTENTS

Day 1 "Foundation" 9
Day 2 "Leadership" 12
Day 3 "Get Away and Listen to God" 15
Day 4 "Game Plan" 18
Day 5 "Being Stable" 20
Day 6 "Bible Reading" 22
Day 7 "O That Men Would Praise Him" 24
Day 8 "Man Cave" 26
Day 9 "When Men Pray" 28
Day 10 "It's Not over Yet" 30
Day 11 "Be Not Weary" 32
Day 12 "Reputation/ Character A man after Gods Heart" 34
Day 13 "Role Model" 37
Day 14 "Trusting God" 39
Day 15 "Be Not Weary" PT 2 41
Day 16 "Audible" 43
Day 17 "Role Model", Part 2 45
Day 18 "The Word of God" 48

Day 19 "Training Day" 51
Day 20 "The World Needs Godly 'Fathers'" 53
Day 21 "Another Chance" 56
Day 22 "Come Back to Church" 58
Day 23 "Respect, Leading Women" 60
Day 24 "Men, Time is of Essence" 62
Day 25 "After Gods Heart" 64
Day 26 "Don't Give Up" 66
Day 27 "Stop Hiding" 69
Day 28 Stop Hiding PT2 71
Day 29 "Men of Integrity" 74
Day 30 The Last Day "Authority" 76

ACKNOWLEDGEMENTS & REFLECTIONS

Because of the plethora of friends I've been blessed with, I find this part to be the most rewarding. I have been blessed with so many wonderful people that have poured into me, so I will try my best to love them. If I have forgotten someone, please forgive me and know that it's not on purpose.

First and foremost thank God for giving me the vision and allowing me to see it through. I want to thank my beautiful wife, Elect Lady Evangelist Barbara Goodson YOU'RE THE BEST! Chaplain Barbara Trawick; thank you for your assistance. To all of my brothers and sisters, I love you guys. To my sister Evangelist Kee, you always encourage me. My parents Nathaniel Goodson Sr. and Ruth Goodson; I love you to life. To my mentor Dr. Leonard Lovett; thanks for pouring into me; I salute you. To my leaders; Keystone Jurisdiction Prelate Bishop VI Prioleau.

Thank you to my great friend and mentor Bishop Darrel Hines and my buddies; Elder Ty Jersey, Elder Jeffrey Nock, and special friend Karen Scott. Supt Greg Frison, Dr. Albert Thompson; special thanks to Mother Denise Marshall. To the Church of God in Christ Commonwealth Jurisdiction, I love you guys forever brothers. Thank you Evang Vernell my pastors' aide president simply the best !!! Hey Supt Charles Giddins, hey Elder Trina Scott. Bishop Sease and Chosen Generation cogic the greatest church in the world, heyyy Karen Warren !!!!! To Heaven's best; Dr. Swinson and my hero and daughter Bryanna... How's Heaven. I dedicate this book in memory of my dad Nathaniel Goodson Sr, Dr. Leonard Lovett, Bishop B Ravenel.

DAY 1

"Foundation"

Matthew 7:24

"Therefore whosoever heareth these sayings of mine, and doeth them, I will liken him unto a wise man, which built his house upon a rock:"

Men, we must understand the importance of a strong foundation, because of the responsibilities and burdens that we carry. There are times when we need to be sure of the foundation. Remember there's a lot of ware and tare, on this old temple (must maintain until he comes back). Ask the Lord to sure up the foundation until the day of redemption. Talk to God and tell him what areas in your life that need to be renewed. Remember verse *24* states: "Whosoever", that means you and me.

The Bible records a story about a man who built his home on sand, and one who built his home on rocks. When the rain descended, the floods came, and the winds blew upon both houses. The house built upon the rock withstood the storm. The house built upon sand did not stand as the rain descended, the floods came, and the winds blew. Why do you ask? The house built on sand was not built on a solid foundation. With a strong foundation you can endure tough times, make better decisions, and be better leaders.

Men, what more can you do to sure up your Foundation?

Notes

DAY 2

"Leadership"

Psalm 37:23

"The steps of a good man are ordered by the Lord: and he delighteth in his way."

We have been created by God to lead. Leading can be exhibited in many ways. We can lead by our talk and by our walk. You may be a loud leader or a quiet leader. Leadership has many looks. To be an effective leader, a leader understands that the leader must first be led. Follow Jesus, and you will an effective leader.

The Bible affirms the steps of a righteous man are ordered by the Lord. Men we must allow God to lead us, so we can lead our families. Remember a good leader was once a good follower. The leader was once led. The Bible states in "all thy ways acknowledge him and he shall direct thy path"

There was a childhood game we played called to follow the leader, remember that game? One had to follow and do everything the leader did. The key to that game was that you had to keep an eye on the leader.

Men, are you keeping an eye on Jesus who is the leader? If you keep an eye on Jesus, then you will be great leaders. The Bible states in Proverbs 3:6 "In all thy ways acknowledge him, and he shall direct thy path." We were made to be leaders it's in our DNA. God will lead you to become leaders.

What leader has made a great impact on your life?

Notes

DAY 3

"Get Away and Listen to God"

Psalm 40:1

"I waited patiently for the LORD; and he inclined unto me, and heard my cry."

Men this is paramount that we hear the voice of God. There are times when you need to find that get-away place. Just you and God. That place that the old church called your "Secret closet". A place where it's just you and God. One on One.

The bible talks about Jesus having a secret place to talk with God. Jesus would often seek that intimate place or secret closet where he would get away from everybody and commune with God, due to the overwhelming responsibilities and demands placed on men. There must be a get-away to listen to God. Jesus would go to the garden, a place where he could get away from the people, to listen and commune with GOD. Brothers find that place, that quiet place and listen to God and "in all thy ways acknowledge him and he will direct your path."

Every year I have a retreat for the men a time when we can get away and commune with God. When we get away we don't have a lot of demands and responsibilities to distract us.

Do you have a quiet place to get away and listen to God?

Notes

DAY 4

"Game Plan"

Proverb 3:6

*"In all thy ways acknowledge him,
and he shall direct thy path."*

Men, we must have a GAME plan, some order, and some direction in our lives. In sports language, this is called the Game plan. No team goes against their opponent without a game plan. Because of the great demand place in your life, there must be a game plan. The Bible reminds us that "the steps of a good man are ordered by the Lord."

The game plan starts with Jesus when God created the world—there was a game plan, and he saw that it was good. Ask God to give you a good game plan and he will direct your path. Never plan without praying and seeking the approval of Jesus. No one can game plan like Jesus. Now understand the devil will try and distort your plan—he's the enemy. So if God gave it to you then the enemy will lose.

Men, what's the Game Plan God Gave You?

Notes

DAY 5

"Being Stable"

James 1:8

"A double minded man is unstable in all his ways."

The Bible affirms that a double-minded man is unstable in all his ways. Gentleman, as we continue in our daily devotions, let us be reminded that God expects us to be stable conscious. To be double-minded is something that the devil will try and afflict men with.

Brothers, we must develop consistency in our walk with the Lord. Men function when they stay in the course. The scripture states a double-minded man is unstable in all his ways. Either you are one way or the other. An unstable man is moving in all kinds of directions. Remain faithful and steadfast always abiding in the work of the Lord.

Brother, God has a plan for you!
Do you know what your plan is?

Notes

DAY 6

"Bible Reading"

Psalm 1:1

"Blessed is the man that walketh not in the counsel of the ungodly, nor standeth in the way of sinners, nor sitteth in the seat of the scornful."

How many times have you opened the box and directions was right there for you to read, to put the item together. But for one reason or another, you just didn't follow the directions, and we ended messing up or starting all over again. Brothers the Bible, the logos, the holy ret is a must-read—it's our compass for life.

Reading the Bible also increases our faith. The Bible states: "So then faith cometh by hearing and hearing by the word of God (Roman 10:17.) The Bible reads in Psalms 130:5: "I wait for the Lord, my soul doth wait, and in his word I do hope." Every day starts with your devotion time of prayer and Bible study, with the Lord. Jesus speaks to us through his word in Psalm 1:2 which affirms that a man who is blessed is one who delights in the Lord and stays in the word of God. In the book, I wrote *"Win the Men"*, I talked about Psalm 1 as being a man's chapter. Read the whole chapter men and it will bless you.

What's your Favorite Scripture and Why?

Notes

DAY 7

"O That Men Would Praise Him"

Acts 16:25

"And at midnight Paul and Silas prayer, and sang praises unto God: and the prisoners heard them."

Men we have allowed the enemy to take away something paramount in being men it's called PRAISE. At my church in Philadelphia, the men have taken to praise. I believe, when a man praises God it shakes the very foundation of heaven, for he inhabits the praise.

There should be a time when men take the lead in praise. Praise comes from the Hebrew word "yadah" meaning an act of homage. When we praise Jesus, we are proclaiming, showing homage, lifting him up.

There are times when our praise will take us through, hold us up, and encourage us. When men praise God, it intimidates the devil. So let the praise began!!!

How Often Do you Praise God?

Notes

DAY 8

"Man Cave"

Psalm 91:1

"He that dwelleth in the secret place of the most high Shall abide under the shadow of the Almighty"

There is a hang out for men that have come on the scene over the past few years called "Man Cave". It's that place or room that was created or refurbished for men who decided, I need a room that I can call my own get-away.

My room that I decorated and designed it's a manly room. Well, men, there's nothing wrong with your own "Man Cave". But, we as men of God need to make sure that when we put together that "Man Cave", make sure your man cave is also your prayer room.

God Bless your man Cave, a place where you can root for your favorite team. Most of all, a place where you can Praise God. So go ahead and enter into His courts with Praise.

Do you have a man-cave, a place of prayer and devotion?

Notes

DAY 9

"When Men Pray"

Acts 12:5

"Peter therefore was kept in prison: but prayer was made, without ceasing of the church unto God for him."

Men, I believe that when a man prays, it shakes the very foundation of Glory. The Bible states men should always pray without ceasing "1 Thessalonians 5:17". Men we must return to praying.

John Wallace states*: "Prayer moves the hand which moves the world."* When men pray great things to happen. When Moses prayed a rock became a water fountain. When Jesus prayed on Calvary sin lost its stain, the grave became a sleeping bag. Men when you pray for things to happen.

One of the greatest impacts on my life was at a young age. I saw my father pray, and it changes my life. Brothers, let's start praying. Men Need It!!!

"Prayer Changes Things"

Do you have a prayer time?

Notes

DAY 10

"It's Not over Yet"

1 Samuel 30, 18

There's a saying, a quote we have heard especially in sports "that it's not over until the fat lady sings", meaning that don't quit until it's over.

Men, I want to encourage you today, despite what you might be going through, it's not over. Just hold on, keep your faith. How many times have we given up on our team and turn the TV off or left the sports complex early, and listened to the radio to find out while driving home that our team came back, or waking up to the news the next day to find out I should have never turned the TV off, they made a comeback.

Men no matter what you have done, it's not too late. So what are you waiting for? Come on back, seek God for redemption. Don't give up. God works better when you can't.

According to scripture what did David get back?

Notes

DAY 11

"Be Not Weary"

Galatians 6:9

"And let us not be weary in well doing: for in due season we shall reap, if we faint not."

I'm writing this while being weary. I'm trying to get to that place of not getting weary in well-doing. I love another translation (the message bible). So let's not allow ourselves to get fatigued doing well. At the right time, we will harvest a good crop if we don't give up or quit.

Now in both translations, it states "Don't get weary, or fatigued in doing good." So fellas in all the good you're doing and not feeling the love, not getting the support, haters hating, listen, don't get weary. By writing this I think I'm there. I know my season is approaching. I will not give up. With all the responsibilities we have, don't get weary. Help is on the way—Jesus

Men don't give up your right there your blessing is there for you

When it gets tough how do you handle it?

Notes

DAY 12

"Reputation/ Character A man after Gods Heart"

2 Corinthians 5:17

"Therefore if any man be in Christ, he is a new creature: old things are passed away; behold all things are become new."

King David has been dubbed, "A man after God's Heart What a reputation to have. Men, your reputation precedes you before you even show up. Your reputation beat you there. Understand Gentleman, we are talking about reputation, not character.

Reputation is what you are supposed to be, the character is what you are. What's your reputation in the body of Christ? Now you know what it was before you accepted Jesus. Once we accept Jesus our reputation should change.

The Bible affirms old things are passed away. People TEND to judge you by one act and pen you with that reputation. Reputation is made in a moment. Character is built in a lifetime as you begin to live for Jesus. Your whole being is changed. Your reputation will change and your character will change. Are you a MAN after God's heart?

How has your reputation change?

NOTES

DAY 13

"Role Model"

Matthew 5:16

*"Let your light so shine before men,
that they may see your good works,
and glorify your Father which is in heaven."*

I think you might agree with me that there are not many role models like there once was. When I was a young fella, I was in awe of men like: "Dr. Martin Luther King", John F Kennedy, my Overbrook Pal Coach. Mason, Bishop O. T. Jones Jr., and Dr. Leonard Lovett. Most of all, my father Nathaniel Goodson, Sr. they were the role models in my life.

Today there are some role models around, just not the way it was. Men, we cannot allow some rappers or sports player to take our place and become the role model. I think a strong Christian man should be a role model. Paul writes: "follow me as I follow Christ." What a message. So, gentlemen as we follow Christ, others will follow us. What an example of Jesus Christ himself.

Who was your role model?
And what can you do to be a better role model?

Notes

DAY 14

"Trusting God"

Proverbs 3:5, 6

*"Trust in the Lord with all thine heart; and
lean not unto thine own understanding.
In all thy ways acknowledge him, and he shall direct thy paths."*

One of the areas in the lives of men that we need to pray for is "trust." Because of the responsibilities that men carry, trusting God is very important in the lives of men. Trusting has always become a shortcoming in the lives of men. It's hard for a man to trust anyone.

This is where your faith in Jesus comes in. Once you develop a relationship with the Lord Jesus you will "begin" to trust again. So, ask God to help you to trust again. But you first must trust in Jesus. The Bible affirms trust in the Lord with all thy heart. Then the Holy Spirit will direct you to people you can trust. The Bible affirms be still and KNOW that I am GOD.

How can you learn to trust Jesus?

Notes

DAY 15

"Be Not Weary" PT 2

Galatians 6:9

"And let us not be weary in well doing: for in due season we shall reap, if we faint not."

The Bible reminds us to "Be not weary in well-doing, for in due season ye shall reap if you faint not." What an encouraging scripture for men in these times that we are living in, we need all the encouragement we can get.

Let's also encourage one another; no one can encourage a man like another man. So gentleman no matter how difficult it gets be encouraged, and yes there are times when we are down to one last strike, but hold on.

God reminds us that there is a reward if we hold on. Notice what the verse reminds us of, it says in **"Due Season."** Your season is approaching. Just maintain until it gets here. I feel strong about this Lesson because on day 11 we talked about the same subject Just hold on, here comes your season thank you, Jesus!!!!!!!!!!!!!!!

What should we do while waiting for our season?

Notes

DAY 16

"Audible"

Proverbs 3:6

"In all thy ways acknowledge him, and he shall direct thy paths."

There are situations in football when the quarterback must change the play right there on the spot. He believes that according to what he sees from the opposing team, he needs to change the play.

There are times when you see the devil is coming at a certain time, in a certain way, and at a certain place. Well, when this happens we must be ready to make a spiritual "audible." How . . . By praying the right prayer, and reading the right scripture. There's a verse in the Bible for just about any situation we are in, and the Holy Spirit will lead you to pray the right prayer for any God-given situation.

Men let us listen to Coach Jesus Christ. God is our coach, and remember he has never lost a game. What a winning streak, the Bible affirms. "In all thy appointed time I'll wait until my change comes."

Whats your next move against the wiles of the devil?

Notes

DAY 17

"Role Model", Part 2

2 Timothy 2:1

*"Thou therefore, my son,
be strong in the grace that is in Christ Jesus"*

I remember some years ago when NBA Basketball star, Charles Barkley stated that he's not a role model even though he's a professional basketball player and watched by a lot of kids and young men. Men, we must become that role model to our little brothers, especially to those who don't have fathers.

I don't want rappers and sports players to be role models for my sons and daughters. It should be men of God. Let's be the role model God wants us to be. Let's live the scripture. Paul states "Follow me as I follow Christ." Now that's a role model. Jesus is the ultimate role model.

My father, Deacon Nathaniel Goodson Sr., was the best role model in my life. Officer Claude Mason was a role model for me. Officer Earl Harris, young men need someone positive they can look up to, someone who is following Jesus. For example, in the Bible Paul was a mentor and role model to Titus; and Moses was a mentor and role model to Joshua. The need is soooo great today because many young men are growing up without Godly role models.

How Can You Be a Godly Role Model?

Notes

DAY 18

"The Word of God"

2 Timothy 2:15

Study to show thyself approved unto God, a workman that needeth not to be ashamed, rightly dividing the word of truth."

In my previous publication "**Win the Men**" I write about in Chapter 1 in Psalms. I call that chapter a Man's Chapter. It opens with blessed is the man. Read that chapter when you get a chance. It will bless your soul.

What's your favorite chapter in the Bible? Men we must read and study the word of God. For every area of life, and the situation there's a scripture. What I love about the word of God is that it has so many stories. The late Bishop O.T. Jones Jr. taught me that if you learn the stories of the Bible, then you have learned the message of the Bible. The Bible is full of stories, which includes the greatest story ever told: Jesus died on the cross, and on the third day he got up with all power in his hand.

What a story, make it a habit of reading your Bible it will help us, it will guide us, and it will keep us. David stated: " . . . thy word have I hid in my heart that I might sin against thee." Study God's word.

What's Your Favorite Scripture and Why?

Notes

DAY 19

"Training Day"

2 Timothy 2:24

"And the servant of the Lord must not strive; but be gentle unto all men, apt to teach, patient."

On day 18 of this devotional, we talked about being a role model. Well, I want to challenge you some more in addition to being a role model—become a trainer. Proverbs 22:6 reads: "Train up a child in the way he should go and when he is old, he will not depart from it." Men let's be trainers. Let's train our children how to be young men and young women of God.

Now understand when I talk about training and raising, we're not talking about just bringing them to church and call it training. It goes far beyond that. There are a lot of people who were brought up in the church and turned out to be evil—Hitler, and Stalin for example.

Training involves spending time, communicating, teaching and praying which is some of the most important tools in training.

What kind of biblical training can you provide?

Notes

DAY 20

"The World Needs Godly 'Fathers"

2 Chronicles 17:3

"And the Lord was with Jehoshaphat, because he walked in the first ways of his father David, and sought not unto Baalim;"

This is a story about a young boy whose father left home when he was young. His father did not play a role in his life. He would often make broken promises and no longer spent time with him. As a result, the son became angry and rebellious. His mother tried everything to raise him, but she couldn't provide what the father could.

God Bless all single mothers, you're awesome!!! The son needed his father. Men we have been created by God to be fathers, naturally and spiritually, our sons and daughters need us. The Bible affirms "Raise a child in the way they should go."

Now the best father is a Godly father. We learn from our heavenly father how to be a father. We need a Godly father, but most of all we need our heavenly father, Jesus Christ. Reach out to our young people who don't have a father in their life: pray with them, read the word of God with them, and most of all—be there for them.

What makes a father a godly father?

Notes

DAY 21

"Another Chance"

Matthew 19:16

"And, behold, one came and said unto him, Good Master, what good thing shall I do, that I may have eternal life?"

I once preached a message entitled "Put me back in the game." The message of this sermon was, even when we mess up; God will give us another chance.

When I was younger, I played basketball for Coach Mason who was my mentor also. There was a time when I played a bad game and he took me out of the game. I felt bad and hurt but I knew he was right. Well, I went to practice and worked harder than ever hoping for another chance to get back in the game. The coach gave me another chance in our next game and boy was I ready.

Sometimes a step back is a step up. There may be times when we may fall, "men" let's get back up and work harder so we can get back in the game. I guarantee you Coach Jesus will give you "another chance." Stop complaining; get ready to go back into the game of life. Prepare yourself!

Are you ready? How did you get ready?

Notes

DAY 22

"Come Back to Church"

Psalm 122:1

*"I was glad when they said unto me,
Let us go into the house of the Lord."*

In my previous publication "Win the Men", there is a chapter called "His Place in the Church." Men, it's important that we find our place in the church. I'm troubled when I hear about men leaving the church. I'm praying that men find their way back to the church. I do believe that we are at the point of a great breakthrough for men.

Men don't give in to the rhetoric that the church is failing. The church is at its strongest when men take the lead. The church is that place where we come together and worship the Lord. Men draw men. Men, there is a place for you in the church. Let's encourage the brethren that there's a place for them in the church. Look out the men are coming back!!!

What can you do to encourage men to come back to the Church?

Notes

DAY 23

"Respect, Leading Women"

Proverbs 12:4

"A virtuous woman is a crown to her husband: but she that maketh ashamed is as rottenness in his bones."

Men let's raise the banner in relationships to treating the ladies. It seems like there's a lot of disrespect toward women today. Some songs degrade and disrespect the women we know. Even young men find it easy to disrespect women.

When Jesus was on the cross he paused the hand of death to provide security for his mother by the way of the disciple John. Men, we must show our little brothers and sons how to respect women and be the leaders that we are called to be. The ladies that we know are looking for Godly leaders. They are looking for men that will respect them and pray with them.

We as men can change the culture that we live in if we allow God to lead us. Men, it's time to step up to appreciate, respect, and lead the women. LET'S APPRECIATE everything they do for us and our children. Our women are a gift from God.

What can we do to show appreciation towards women?

Notes

DAY 24

"Men, Time is of Essence"

Colossians 4:5

"Walk in wisdom toward them that are without, Redeeming the time"

Spending time with your family, friends, and most of all God should be a priority in our life. Because of the responsibilities we take on as men, we can easily neglect these three areas in our life.

Early in the morning, the first person that you should spend time with is Jesus. He will give you proper instructions for the day. Great way to get the day running, then you will be able to spend the much needed time with your family and friends.

Proverbs 4:1 affirms "Hear, ye children, the instruction of a father, and attend to know understanding." It takes time to do, hear, instruct, and attend.

Men our time is important, never get too busy for God. The Bible affirms there is a time for everything: Take time with God!

How can you make more time for God?

Notes

DAY 25

"After Gods Heart"

Psalm 51:10

"Create in me a clean heart, O God; and renew a right spirit within me."

David has often been referred to as a man after God's own heart. What a reputation to have. Remember this is the same David who had an extra-marital affair. David had his lover's husband sent to the front line in the battle to be killed. David continued the affair, had a child from this affair until his Pastor Nathan approached him and challenged him to repent.

Men even though we mess up, don't stay there: repent and seek God for change and become a "man after God's own heart. Only through trial, tribulation, sin, and suffering, can we receive such a label.

David repented and was restored, and reconciled back to God. We all have had many labels and reputation. Let's try for that label or reputation of: "A man after God's own heart."

How can we get rid of the negative labels we have?

NOTES

DAY 26

"Don't Give Up"

Galatians 6:9

"And let us not be weary in well doing: for in due season we shall reap, if we faint not."

Have you ever had one of those days when it seems like everything is going wrong? I think we all have these days. One of my favorite encouraging scriptures is Galatians 6:10.

It reminds me that if we stay the course, if we hold on, if we keep our faith, our time of blessings will arrive. There will be times when we want to throw in the towel, just don't give up. There is a reward if we "faint not."

There was a fight years ago between Sugar Ray Leonard and Roberto Duran. In the middle of the fight, Roberto Duran quit by saying those infamous words "No Mas, No Mas" meaning no more no more. He quit, gave up.

No matter what, we must hold on. God promised that he would never leave us or forsake us. We cannot give up on God. Someone once said that quitters never win and winners never quit. Oh yeah

Sugar Ray won the fight. Just hold on and God will help you. I know he can because he did it for me.

AS YOU CAN SEE I LOVE THIS SCRIPTURE WE READ IT IN DAY 11 AND 15. I FEEL THIS TO BE A VERY ENCOURAGING SCRIPTURE FOR MEN

When you need encouragement, what scriptures do you read?

Notes

DAY 27

"Stop Hiding"

Genesis 3:9

"And the Lord God called unto Adam, and said unto him, Where art thou?"

The Bible tells us that, every day God would show up and greet Adam at the peak of dawn. I can imagine Adam would joyfully wait for God to show up, but on this particular day, Adam does not have joy in his step and gleam in his eye. He's trying to avoid God the Father.

Isn't it something when we were little kids when we did something wrong we would try to avoid our dad or mom, not realizing we were giving ourselves away? They could tell by our reactions that we did something wrong.

That's what happened with Adam and Eve. They went into hiding when they knew they had messed up. So instead of greeting God at the doorway of heaven they covered themselves and went into hiding.

Can you hear God asking those bone chilling words? "Adam where art thou?"

What man in the bible tried to hide from God?

Notes

DAY 28

Stop Hiding PT2

Genesis 3: 8-24

"And they heard the voice of the Lord God walking in the garden in the cool of the day: and Adam and his wife hid themselves from the presence of the Lord God amongst the trees of the garden (v8)."

Men, we must come out of hiding. Now there are various ways one can hide, it might be in sex, alcohol, gambling, just to name a few. Remember, we can't hide from God, he's everywhere. The Bible affirms the earth is the lords the psalmist also quotes "If I make my bed in hell thou are there." A famous boxer stated you can run but you can't hide. Be honest with God don't hide from him but run to him he's a forgiving God.

When men go into hiding it often leads to destruction, if you hide in drugs, porn, or any type of addiction it will eventually destroy you. We must come clean, repent, and seek restoration. He is a forgiving God. The Bible affirms come out from amongst them and be ye separated.

There's no place to hide—God is everywhere Jonah tried to hide from God and God allow a whale to swallow him up. After he repented the great whale spit him out and Jonah did what God called him to do. Jonah tried to hide but he couldn't. It's time to accept what God has for you. He wants to use you for kingdom work. Come on BROTHERS, get ready and stop trying to hide— it's your time for God's glory.

Have you read the story of Jonah in the Old Testament?

If not, read it and it will bless you.

NOTES

DAY 29

"Men of Integrity"

Proverbs 10:9

"He that walketh uprightly walketh surely; but he that perverteth his ways shall be known."

The man of integrity walks securely, but he who takes a crooked path will be found out. I looked up the word "integrity" and it is defined as, the concept of consistency of actions, values, methods, measures, principles, expectations, and outcomes.

I found some more, how about this one: Someone who is honest and ethical and has high morals and principles. Men, this is the kind of man that God is looking for, and this country needs.

This verse affirms that a man of integrity walks securely. He has no hidden agenda. He is lead by the Spirit of God. Many men in the Bible were men of integrity. "Joseph" was a man of integrity. I agree with the late great Bishop O.T. Jones, Jr. that Joseph was one of the greatest men in the Bible. He represented integrity and would not comprise.

How Do We Become Men of Integrity?

Notes

DAY 30

The Last Day "Authority"

Well, men, we are on the last day of these thirty-day readings. It's my prayer that you apply the principles and Biblical concepts of these readings to empower you and to live a Godly and spiritual life.

I encourage you to walk in your victory. As men of God, we must exercise the power that we possess—God-given authority. In my book "Authority" "Beyond your Ability", we talk about your God-given authority, not your abilities, but your God-given authority that cannot be explained through human reasoning but through divine authority. God will put you in a place or in situations where all you have is your God-given authority. More of this can be found in my NEW book. "AUTHORITY, BEYOND YOUR ABILITY"

Well, God bless you, Priest. Walk-in your victory and be a spirit-led man.

I pray that you were blessed during these thirty days—Be Bless.

Notes

www.ingramcontent.com/pod-product-compliance
Lightning Source LLC
LaVergne TN
LVHW011739060526
838200LV00051B/3248